School Counselling in Jamaica

by:

Denise N. Fyffe

A Note to the Reader

School or Guidance counsellors are one of the key professionals found in educational institutions. They are there to facilitate more than just the educational needs of a student. Counsellors handle the psychological, mental, and spiritual needs as well. Jamaican guidance counsellors often fill several roles and are used to 'pitching in' where needed.

School Counselling in Jamaica briefly introduces the Jamaican educational system and reaches back into history and highlights the psychometric movement, the trait and factor theory as well as various legislations that impacted the development of present guidelines and ethical standards. The book also examines the various roles and responsibilities of a Guidance Counsellor.

- *Denise N. Fyffe*

School Counselling in Jamaica

Published in the United States by Jamaica Pen Publishers. jamaicapenpublishers.com/publishing

Second Edition

Jamaica Pen Publishers

TABLE OF CONTENT

Acknowledgement

Introduction to Research class with Mr. Louis Moyston was an experience in true upliftment, educationally. He invested time, patience, and sound advice into his students to make sure that they were following the correct procedures, down to the letter. I thank you, Sir Moyston, for the investment into my education and future.

- *Denise N. Fyffe*

School Counselling in Jamaica

HISTORY OF SCHOOL COUNSELLING

Mrs. Goodrich showed up to the Fairies Secondary School as usual, looking forward to the challenges that would greet her in her chosen profession, as a School Counsellor. Her day was particularly hectic and burdensome, as several boys got in trouble for missing classes and gathering at the back of the school and she was expected to 'set di bwoy dem on di straight and narrow', according to the principal. In addition, one of her favourite students, Latoya who was of Muslim background, in her counselling session that afternoon admitted that she would not continue to college, but get a part time job, marry, and have children. Mrs. Goodrich, at the end of the day, sat down, and reflected on the day's occurrences. She began to wonder what she was to do as the school counsellor, and whether there were problems like this 75 years ago. Mrs. Goodrich pondered what would have happened if there were no school counsellors today?

School counselling has changed over the years. It has transformed from a mere larva to the beautiful butterfly that it is today. School or guidance counsellors, as they are called in Jamaica, are "professional members of an educational team who assists students in the personal, social, academic and career development aspects of education through services such as individual and small group counselling and classroom teaching; as well as provide leadership in educational reform (advocacy)." They are traditionally known as a guidance counsellor, although this term is deemed inaccurate by most professionals today.

A Brief History

School Counselling transitioned from the vocational, guidance and counselling movement of the late 19th and early 20th century. It adopted its functions and design from the vocational counselling field and applied it to schools, the formal institutions that 'house' this field today. School Counselling is a relatively new field, compared to other fields of study. It is a process and the rules and guidelines that are the guideposts for it today, were changed in the past, are changing in the present and will continue to evolve in the future.

School counselling branched out of the vocational guidance movement, in the United States at the beginning of the 20th century. This was due to the societal, political, educational, trade and industry developments of the time. Jesse B. Davis is deemed the first to offer a systematic school guidance program, in 1907.

In 1908, the "Father of Vocational Guidance" Frank Parsons, established the Bureau of Vocational Guidance to assist young people in making the transition from school to work. Other pioneers such as David Hill, Anna Reed and Eli Weaver had a different approach as they created guidance services which sought to make students employable.

The 1920s to the 1930s saw ascension in the interest of school counselling and guidance because of the rise of progressive education in schools. There were no set standards that were accepted by all for training and various philosophies were propagated. However, personal, social, and moral developments were accentuated. "Many schools reacted to this movement as anti-educational, saying that schools should teach only the fundamentals of education. This, combined with the economic hardship of the Great Depression, led to a decline in school counselling and guidance" (Wikipedia, 2006).

Psychometric Movement

Alfred Binet and his colleague T. Simon, in 1905, "developed an instrument to measure mental ability. This was used to categorize students according to aptitude in the Paris school system". This practise was adopted by the U.S.A, where standardized tests were utilised to track students according to ability. Psychologists and counsellors were used to select, recruit and train military personnel in the 1940s. This propelled the counselling movement in schools by providing ways to test students and meet their needs. Schools accepted these military tests openly. School counselling advanced to incorporate the use of assessment instruments which stemmed from its use by the military.

Trait and Factor Theory

Theories were developed to support the inclusion of assessment instruments in School Counselling and assisted this field to establish itself further. "The testing movement collided with the vocational guidance movement and what emerged was the 'Trait and Factor Theory' which endorsed the use of diagnostic and standardized assessment to identify individual strengths and preferences, which was used to counsel people about occupations for which they were best suited. [1]" E.G. Williamson was a champion of the trait and factor theory.

Legislation and Acts

In the 1950s, the government of the United States established the Guidance and Personnel Services Section in the Division of State and

---

1 http://cmhs.utoledo.edu/mritchie/Courses/cmhs5010/unit02/history_of_school_counseling.htm

Local School Systems. In 1957, the Soviet Union launched Sputnik I. Out of concern that the Russians were beating the U.S. in the space race, which had military implications and that there were not enough scientists and mathematicians, the American government passed the National Defence Education Act (NDEA), which spurred a huge growth in vocational guidance through large amounts of funding for guidance institutes to train teachers to become guidance counsellors. This movement greatly increased the number of guidance counsellors in schools and established counsellor education programs in universities across the nation. In 1964, NDEA was amended to provide funding for elementary school counsellors. Since the 1960s, the profession of school counselling has continued to grow as new legislation and new professional developments were established to refine and further the profession and improve education (Schmidt, 2003).

As school counselling continued to evolve gradually, persons encouraged that the procedures, conventions, and practices must also change. C. Gilbert Wren wrote 'The Counsellor in a Changing World', in 1962. Passing judgment on high school counsellors, he pointed out that they needed to concentrate their endeavours on career counselling and crisis counselling and supported the emerging new elementary school counsellors to provide developmental guidance services to all children through a comprehensive guidance program.

School counselling was revolutionized by pioneers such as Parsons, Davis, and Alfred Binet and since then guidance counsellors have proliferated throughout American high schools and schools right across the world. Organisations such as Association for

Assessment in Counselling, American College Counselling Association, Association for Counsellors and Educators in Government, Association for Multicultural Counselling and Development, American School Counsellor Association, and the National Career Development Association have been created so that these professionals can be guided by approved professional organisations. As such there has been development in terms of streamlining the guidelines and legislation.

THE EDUCATION SYSTEM

One of the foundational elements of any modern society is education. It bears great responsibility for the development and sustainability of any nation. Education is a formal or informal system developed to assist or direct people into becoming purposeful units which contribute in a positive way to society. Formal education didn't always exist, at least not in the form it is now.

Earlier societies placed more emphasis on working and earning a living than spending many hours or years in a classroom learning a skill. Farming and hunting were the main way of life before our world became industrialized and there were skill intensive jobs. Because of this, people had to be trained to perform certain tasks. In today's world construct, formal education is mandatory and integral in every nation that wishes to establish a thriving economy and equip its citizen with skills that will make them productive contributors and not a menacing burden. From early childhood to adulthood, people are enrolled in educational institutions to learn a basic curriculum and then move on to more advanced and specialized programmes.

Jamaican Education System

According to The Glossary of Education Reform (2014), the term education system generally refers to public schooling, not private schooling, and more commonly to kindergarten through high school programmes. However, in Jamaica, the educational system is segmented into four different levels: namely, Early Childhood, Primary, Secondary and Tertiary. Schools or school districts are typically the smallest recognized form of "education system" and countries are the largest. States are also considered to have education systems. The role of the education system in Jamaica, as stated by the Ministry of Education (MOE), is "to meet the needs for greater self-financing capability, a better definition of Jamaica's educational goals and the expansion of the system to meet both individual and national needs".

To access the first stage of schooling, students enrol in public and private institutions from the ages of three to six (3-6) years of age. Children up to age six access early childhood education through day care centres and basic or prep schools throughout the island. According to the Ministry of Education (MOE), for a student to progress to the Primary level a "Grade One Individual Learning Profile (GOILP) is used to ascertain students' capabilities and mastery of the skills and concepts taught at the Early Childhood level, so that strategies can be developed to advance their learning".

After completing their Early Childhood education, children move on to Primary, Junior High or All-Age institutions. There are over three hundred thousand students in Jamaica's Primary schools, that range from grades one through to six. During their years several tests are administered; these include:

1. Grade 1: Readiness Inventory
2. Grade 3: Assessment tests in Math and Language Arts
3. Grade 4: Literacy Test
4. Grade 6: Achievement Test (GSAT)

When students matriculate to the Primary level of education, they complete six (6) grades and sit the Grade Six Achievement Examination (GSAT) to gain admission to High schools.

In secondary schools, students have the option of going to co-ed schools (both boys and girls) or boys' only and girls' only schools. Generally, in High schools, students complete five (5) more grades. They start from grades seven through to eleven and complete two sets of major exams - one at grade eleven, and if they continue, one at grade thirteen - to move on to tertiary institutions or to the world of work. When students complete their Caribbean Secondary Education Certificate (CSEC) subjects successfully, they then exit with a high school diploma. Some students opt to stay two more years in grades 12 and 13. At this level, they pursue, Sixth Form and sit the Caribbean Advanced Proficiency Examination (CAPE). At this juncture, many students divert to the working world, while others move on to the Tertiary level of the education system.

Tertiary education is accessed through universities, teachers' colleges, and specialized institutions. Over the last two decades, there has been a growth in the number of tertiary institutions operating in Jamaica. The list includes:

- Caribbean Graduate School of Theology
- Caribbean Institute of Business
- Caribbean Institute of Technology (CIT)
- Caribbean Maritime Institute (CMI)
- College of Agriculture, Science and Education (CASE)
- Edna Manley College of the Visual and Performing Arts (an artistic conservatory)
- Excelsior Community College (EXED)
- G.C. Foster College of Physical Education and Sports
- International University of the Caribbean (IUC)
- Jamaica Theological Seminary

- Management Institute for National Development
- Mico University College
- Northern Caribbean University (NCU)
- Pre-University School (Pre-UWI)
- United Theological College of the West Indies
- University College of the Caribbean (UCC)
- University of Technology (U-Tech)
- University of the West Indies at Mona
- Vector Technology Institute
- Vocational Training Development Institute

The Jamaican education system is of great importance, to Jamaica's government. Students who do exceptionally on their exams in primary school are granted scholarships for their high school education. The government, in recent years, subsidized the tuition for every child at the secondary level and exam fee in grade eleven. Millions of dollars are spent annually on back-to-school programs that aid students with tuition costs. Through to adulthood, Jamaica provides institutions that offer quality education to its people.

School Management

Schools are complex organisations that deal with a variety of areas such as curriculum, finance, communication, discipline, record keeping, human resources, other resources, and guidance. It is the type of working environment that requires effective teamwork and effective school management. Teams are essential in handling management control, information gathering, processing of students and information, work distribution and duties. Evidence of teams can be seen through form teachers, head of departments, grade supervisors, etc. It is important that this be maintained as it produces higher levels of productivity in the work environment.

School Organisational Structure

Schools support and serve students. They are there to help and guide the future generation by facilitating the teaching and learning process. It is a demanding function and as such more than one person is needed to see to the day-to-day needs or issues that might arise. The hierarchy, of the schools in Jamaica, is such that they engender effective school management.

Within the school system there are several professionals that are integral to the everyday function of the institution. These include educational administrators such as a principal, vice principals, deans, bursars, others guidance counsellors. Also comprises the teachers, nurse, librarian, office or administrative staff, ancillary staff, technicians and coach or PE teacher. The list is not extensive, and divergent schools will differ in their organisational structure.

Guidance Counsellors

School counsellors are comparatively new additions to the education system landscape; nonetheless, they play an important role in educational institutions. They are there to facilitate more than just the educational needs of a student, but the psychological, mental, and spiritual as well. Jamaican guidance counsellors often fill several roles and are used to pitching in where needed. Still, there is a severe shortage of such professionals when matched with the number of students in any primary, secondary, or tertiary institution in Jamaica. In recent years, the ratio has been quoted as being at 1 to 650 students.

One of the primary services offered by school counsellors is one on one counselling;

this certainly is not possible when you serve more than 500 clients. As such, interpersonal conflicts, educational issues, mental and psychological disorders among the school population will go unnoticed. Counsellors would therefore not be able to recommend behavioural, psychological, and academic evaluations. Guidance counsellors would not be able to execute effective preventative programmes which could help these students.

THE COUNSELLING PROCESS

Counselling is a process. It is a collaborative effort between the counsellor and client. Counsellors work with individuals, families, groups, schools, and other organizations. School counsellors help students identify goals and potential solutions to problems which cause emotional turmoil. They also help students to improve communication and coping skills, to strengthen self-esteem and promote behaviour change and optimal mental health.

Through counselling one can examine their behaviours, thoughts and feelings that are causing difficulties. As such, it is possible to learn effective ways to deal with problems by building upon personal strengths. A professional counsellor will encourage personal growth and development in ways that promote the client's interest and welfare[2].

Rapport

This is the first stage in counselling. Here the counsellor establishes a climate of acceptance, openness, and mutuality by empathizing with the counselee, listening to his problems and feelings, communicating his understandings, and developing a genuine interest in him. In establishing rapport, you attend on the counselee, both physically and psychologically. It is at this stage, that the counselee begins to want to share his feelings.

To establish rapport, you build common ground between you and the client. Listen and be sensitive to the client's style. Listen closely to the client for cues on how you should act. Try to speak with the same rhythm and tone of voice. Make some friendly observation about

---

[2] (http://www.counseling.org)

your surroundings. If the client, makes small talk use this opportunity as small talk can be a simple yet effective way of building rapport and trust. Choose the right conversational topics, such as the other person's area of expertise, news, or movies. However, when you are thinking small talk, be sensitive to the other person's mood and circumstances (Booher, 1999). Be positive and upbeat. Relax and make a connection. It is important to appear open and friendly. Give the client a firm handshake if s/he offers it and remember to smile. Look attentive, with good posture and consistent eye contact. To create a positive first impression, you need to connect immediately regardless of age, gender, ethnic background, mood, or the situation (Mowatt, 2000).

- Importance

Establishing and maintaining rapport is vital for the disclosure of information, the initiation of change, and the ultimate success of counselling.

Assessment

This is the stage of integrative understanding, when you are piecing together all the themes you heard at the previous stage. This process involves the collection and classification of information related to the client's personhood and reasons for seeking counselling (Hackney and Cormier, 1996). It is at this stage (a) when you will use leading responses and (b) find that the Counselee begins to realize his real problems and gets a realistic perception of himself, because the Counsellor will be helping him to examine all ramifications of problem/s and to identify and examine the connected behavioural themes. Clarify, prioritise problems; Clarify circumstances related to problem; Explore development of problem; Discuss feelings, thoughts about problem; Explore client's construction of reality Explore client's relationships; Identify goals for change.

For the Counselee - it is the actual stage of self-understanding. He now perceives his self-system, his problem areas, how he interacts with others, his strengths, and his weaknesses, and he may even see his untapped strengths in the process. He also learns from the Counsellor to piece together his behavioural patterns and to examine all ramifications of a problem. The Counselee now gets an objective understanding of himself and realizes and appreciates the need for change.

- Importance

This stage is key as it determines how the counsellor will proceed in the following stages. Without it the goal setting stage would be futile as it identifies the problem to be addressed. It is important to attempt to assess problems in more than one way to avoid the constraints of personal bias or theoretical encapsulation. The problem should be considered in the client's context as well as a theoretical context (Hackney and Cormier, 1996).

Goal - Setting

Based on the Counselee's understanding of himself, the Counsellor will help to work out specific action programmes chosen by the Counselee. The Counsellor will collaborate with him to change some of the Counselee's behaviour or to help change the environment to suit the Counselee's specific action programmes to be worked out.

It could be to help develop coping mechanisms or to take remedial action to make good any behavioural deficits such as lack of assertiveness or to get over temper outbursts. Thus, the Counsellor, as a more mature and developed person, collaborates with the

Counselee, to bring about constructive change whilst giving support to his chosen constructive action plan. It is goal-directed at this stage, and the Counsellor will involve the Counselee in target setting. The counsellor may do several tasks in this stage namely: Set and periodically review change goals; Conceptualise problem; Design an intervention plan; Design an evaluation plan.

For the Counselee - it is learning process and training in decision - making aimed at living a more effective life; by equipping himself with the ability to solve problems, identity and solve future problems, change some of his problem behaviour, and in that way work towards achieving the Counselee's goals.

o Importance

Setting goals is very important to the success of counselling. Why are goals so important? The best answer is a simple one.

We set goals to know how well counselling is working and when counselling should be concluded (Hackney and Cormier, 1996).

Initiation Interventions

Intervention can be viewed as encouraging clients to recognise and assume personal responsibility for their choices. All counsellors have a therapeutic plan that they follow, a plan that is related to the assessment of the presenting problem, to their view of human nature and change processes, and to the resulting goals that have been agreed upon (Hackney and Cormier, 1996).

A major issue of intervention is change, as the main objective of counselling is to initiate and facilitate desirable change. Choosing the right intervention is a process of adaptation. Not all interventions work for all clients, or as well as one might predict. Sometimes the 'perfect' intervention turns out to be perfectly awful (Hackney and Cormier, 1996). The plan of action in this stage is not set in stone and can be revisited as the counsellor evaluates progress.

- Importance

If there is no plan of action or intervention then this defeats the purpose of a counselling session, which is change. If no intervention takes place, then the client will be stuck at the same state he or she came in with, at the rapport stage.

Termination

This could be closure for the day or the final Counselling Interview. If it is closure for the day, the Counsellor will summarise what was discussed up to that time and fix the date for the next meeting. At the beginning of the interview the next day, the Counsellor will make it a point to go over all that again, for reasons of communication accuracy and for monitoring purposes. If it is termination of counselling too, everything discussed (Reviewing problem and effects of intervention) will be gone over with the Counselee. Termination of the counselling relationship is a natural process, which both counsellor and client decide that the relationship should end (George and Cristiani, 1995). Additionally, the Counsellor should make the Counselee understand, that s/he is always welcome to see the Counsellor again, if so desired.

For the Counselee - it is greater self-understanding and greater self-confidence. If it is termination of Counselling, he should have identified and changed his inappropriate behaviour, equipped himself with sound decision-making ability, and above all, developed a positive self-concept.

- Importance

It is imperative that the counsellor acknowledges how important s/he is to the client and how their actions affect them. One of the initial rules is that no harm be done to the client. Therefore, this stage should be dealt with using sensitivity, with intentionality and forethought.

Termination may present the greatest challenge as the client may or may not want to end his or her relationship with the counsellor. They have grown so dependent on this individual who have assisted them for a particular duration. What the counsellor may do is to let the termination stage last for several sessions and mention it about the four - six sessions ahead. This will allow the stage of denial to run its course if it occurs. All counsellors will have different experiences with their clients and so need to implement various termination techniques.

COUNSELLING AND PSYCHOTHERAPY TECHNIQUES

In this section, three theoretical approaches to counselling and psychotherapy used by counsellors will be examined. They include, Gestalt therapy, posited by Frederick (Fritz) Perls with a theory base in individual psychology categorized under existential-humanistic theories; transactional analysis, posited by Eric Berne with a theory base in transactional analysis categorized under Cognitive-Behavioural theories; and Adlerian therapy posited by Alfred Adler with a theory base in individual psychology categorized under psychodynamic theories.

These theories possess major differences in their approaches, but have similarities, which enable the counsellor to use them, especially when counselling clients using a multicultural approach to counselling. We will look at the similarities and the differences in these three theoretical approaches to counselling then show how the Adlerian theory suites the Jamaican Career counselling situation.

Gestalt Therapy

According to Capuzzi and Gross (2004), the central ideas of the theory state that - Gestalt Counsellors and psychotherapists strive to encompass the whole organism and operate from the perspective that human beings have the capacity and strength to grow, develop and become the persons they want to be. Similarly Gladding (2004) in explaining the theory states that human beings work for wholeness and completeness of life and that each person has a self-actualising tendency that emerges through personal interaction with the environment and the beginning of self-awareness. Some basic assumptions about this theory are - individuals can deal with their life problems if they are fully aware of what is happening in their environment; holism is crucial, that is, the concept of unifying wholes, which includes mind and body, past and present, and individual and environment; the idea that the here and now is most important as it is the present rather than the past or future which is necessary for promoting the growth process (Capuzzi and Gross, 2003). The role of the Gestalt counsellor then is to create an atmosphere that promotes a client's exploration of what is needed to grow by being intensely and personally involved with clients and being honest with the counselling goal emphasising the here and now and recognition of the immediacy of the issues or situation (Gladding, 2003).

Transactional Analysis

The central theme of Transactional Analysis (TA), posited by Eric Berne, is that each man and woman have a multiple nature concentrating on the essential conviction that each one of us has parts of our personality which surface and affect our behaviour according to different circumstances. These three alter ego states: Parent, Adult, and Child - have different definitions than in standard language. Parent is our; 'Taught' concept of life; Adult is our 'Thought' concept of life and Child is our 'Felt' concept of life. When we communicate, we are doing so from one of our own alter ego states, our Parent, Adult or Child. When two people encounter each other, one of them will speak to the other; this is called the Transaction Stimulus. The reaction from the other person he called the Transaction Response. The person sending the Stimulus is called the Agent. The person who responds is called the Respondent. TA became the method of examining the transaction wherein: 'I do something to you, and you do something back.

TA is a social psychology and a method to improve communication underpinned by the philosophy that: people can change and have a right to be in the world and be accepted. There is a certain connection between mind and body, that is, the link between the biological and the psychological, of which an example is a psychological fear of spiders and a biological feeling of nausea.

Eric Berne proposed that the human brain acts like a tape recorder, and whilst we may 'forget' experiences, the brain still has them recorded. According to Chapman (2005), Eric Berne stated that a contract is "an explicit bilateral commitment to a well-defined course of action." Chapman further explained that this means that all parties need to agree, why they want to do something, with whom, what they are going to do, and how it will be done. Our feelings at the time determine which one we use, and at any time something can trigger a shift from one state to another. When we respond, we are also doing this from one of the three states, and it is in the analysis of these stimuli and responses that the essence of Transactional Analysis rests. Therefore, TA is a contractual approach wherein the counsellor must teach the client how to communicate, create contracts with the client for change, at the same time instructing the TA language.

Adlerian Theory

The central idea of the Adlerian Theory is that people are primarily motivated by social interest, that is, a feeling of being connected with the society as a part of the social whole. In other words, the theory focuses on social interests as well as the purposefulness of behaviour. According to Gladding (2004), the major tenets of this theory are that people strive to become successful. There is a tendency for each person to feel inferior to others and people are influenced by future goals and past cause. Persons who have or share ordinal birth position may have more in common than siblings from the same family. Also, people create a style of life by age five that is, three main life tasks, which includes society, work, and sexuality. Developing social interest, contributing to society, spirituality or coping with self, work is essential for human survival and that interdependence must be learnt are also assumptions.

While the counsellor's primary focus should concern diagnosis and teaching the client about what lifestyles are healthy or holistic, she should also establish an equalitarian relationship with the client, which should remain therapeutic in nature (Gladding, 2003).

Similarities and Differences

The theories differ in many ways. The Transactional Analysis theory (Cognitive-

Behavioural Theory) philosophical base and key concepts are cognitive, analytical, contractual, interpersonal as well as the social-interactive and awareness elements, which are involved in psychotherapy process. Based on the concepts of the theory the view of human nature is that people can change; this is an optimistic view; which also stresses the importance of intrapersonal integration and analyses of transactions. The key concepts or philosophical base of Gestalt theory is the focus of existential concepts, here, and now, awareness, emphasis on client as well as its confrontational method. Existential because it focuses on the meaning of life that is, people form their lives by the choices they make. This theory's views are that human beings work for wholeness and completeness in life. It also stresses the inner wisdom of persons and discusses the importance of change. Finally, the Adlerian theory, which is a psychodynamic theory philosophical base and key concepts, are holistic, phenomenological, and socially orientated as well as teleology. For the Adlerian theory, the primary motivator is social interest. Emphasis is also placed on birth order, family, lifestyles, teleology, as well as the influence of goals on personal growth and development. When the concepts are carefully examined, the major differences can be seen or examined from the perspective of the role and goal of the counsellor in the approaches to psychotherapy.

The role of the counsellor when using Transactional Analysis (TA) therapy is to act as a teacher, and to build contracts with clients for change. Whereas the counsellor's role when using Gestalt therapy, according to Capuzzi and Gross (2004), to create an atmosphere that promotes clients to explore what is needed to change, thus emphasizing one of the key concepts, the importance of change. In addition, the emphasis on "here and now" helps the client to recognize patterns in his/her life that need to be changed now. So, even though the goal of each theory is to create change, the counsellor who uses TA therapy integrates the use of a contract whereas Gestalt counsellors use what is happening in the environment as well as what is in the present rather than on the past. When the role of the Adlerian counsellor is scrutinized the counsellor is in an equilateral relationship with clients. The counsellor acts as a model as well as a teacher; thus he/she shares hunches as well as providing encouragement and assigning homework. So, the role of the Adlerian Counsellor is different from Gestalt and TA as the counsellor and client have equal responsibility. In addition, transference is encouraged by Adlerian therapy.

The difference can also be seen regarding the goal of each theory. The goals of TA are transformation, attainment of health and autonomy as well as increase the awareness of clients. However, the goal of Gestalt theory is to identify themes that are central to the client's self-organization, also, to emphasise the here and now, recognition of the immediacy. In addition, focus is on non-verbal and verbal expressions and resolving of the past to be integrated in the future. On the other hand, is the Adlerian theory, its goal is different from TA and Gestalt theory as its emphasis is on social interest, correction of faulty assumptions and mistaken goals. So, based on the information outlined, the goals of each theory differ.

Therefore, overall functions of Cognitive-Behavioural theory (TA) are to enable clients to function well regarding the environment and to use more socially desirable behaviours. On the other hand, the main function of Existential-humanistic theory (Gestalt) is moving the client toward self-direction, self-awareness, and improved decision-making. Clients are helped to trust their own capabilities and assume responsibility for all aspects of their lives. Finally, the main trust of the psychodynamic theory is an acknowledgement of client's past development and histories that are important to help them discover the unconscious roots of the present.

According to Gibson and Mitchell (1999), Gestalt theory places emphasis on the self-actualising of individuals. Therefore, it helps persons to reach their fullest potential. In a similar way Adlerian theory outlines that people strive to become successful thus emphasizing the connection between self-actualising and success. In addition, Adlerian theory also posits that family environment is important to a person's development. This point is supported by Transactional Analysis (TA) theory, which views normal personality as a product of a healthy personality. These two theories are similar since they disclose the impact of the family or parenting on the development of a healthy personality. Gestalt theory promotes the holism concept - mind and body, similarly TA seeks to understand the different personalities that are a part of us. Therefore, the Gestalt theory takes into consideration all aspect of the person and TA theory also take in consideration all the different personality, to fully understand individuals. Finally, as regards to the limitations of the theories, the Gestalt and TA theories are said to lack strong theoretical base.

The Adlerian theory often referred to as Individual Psychology perceive the person or client holistically thus focusing on the uniqueness of such individuals. Adler believes that people are primarily motivated by social interest or the feeling of being associated to society as part of the social whole. The theory assumes that people strive to become successful, are influenced by experiences and future goals, the family environment is important to a person's development and people tend to feel inferior to others. It posits that person's birth position have more in common with others from the same birth position than those who do not. Believing people have a social interest to contribute to society, the Adlerian theory suggest the learning of interdependence through three main life tasks, namely work, society, and sexuality.

It is with these assumptions as our basis of thought that we believe the Adlerian theory is best suited to the Jamaican Career Counselling situation. In the Jamaican circumstance it is observed that people strive to become successful, whether it is positive or otherwise. It is a collective belief that status symbols such as house, luxury cars and high paying jobs or those that carry status are benchmarks for success. If these targets are not achieved persons usually feel inadequate and may operate daily or perform at work poorly. These individuals may also seek to attain different jobs or may come to a crossroads of indecision. Therefore, it is the career counsellor's job or main objective to respond and assist this individual from the perspective of educating the client and transitioning from this position. This may take the form of advising them to study further, gather new career skills, learn to budget or just to accept themselves for who they are; these link to the Adlerian psychotherapy technique of Encouragement.

Another aspect of Adler's theory is that of individuals being influenced by future goals and past causes. People tend to learn from the examples and way of life set by their parents, family, or peers. They may feel inferior to others if they do not measure up to expected achievements. It is almost endemic in our society for persons to plan and save for the future whether it is through the credit union, bank accounts, saving schemes or the informal method of 'partner'. Gone are the days where our parents would work all their lives to procure houses and cars. Now an individual can save a certain percentage and pay the balance within a five-to-40-year period. This allows them to realize their goals much sooner. Where individuals have a perceived faulty lifestyle the career counsellor will help them to overcome it, by utilising techniques such as Task Setting and 'Acting as if'. These allow the individual to set short-term goals and realise himself or herself as the person who they see themselves as in their dreams.

The family environment is important to a person's development; this is one of the main tenets of the Adlerian theory. Family members provide support; whether financial, physical, psychological, or emotional. They can also be the stumbling block in a person's path if this is done negatively or the support is just not provided. Where families are separated or lead by a single parent (usually the female), persons are forced to join the workforce at an earlier age, surpassing a higher level of education or training and settling for jobs which provide them with low job satisfaction. It now becomes the Counsellors duty to assume the role of teacher through psychotherapy techniques of the Adlerian perspective, such as 'Push button' where clients are encouraged to realise, they have choices about what stimuli (family?) they pay attention to.

Career counselling in Jamaica is rather a new phenomenon, having its basis in schools and other academic institution. The forms of counselling practised are designed to help persons develop their educational, social, personal, and career strengths. These programs focus on needs, interest, and values of everyone with a commitment to individual uniqueness and the maximum development of human potential. The authors of this paper assume that utilising the Adlerian method of psychotherapy fits into the already established codes and standards of current practises in Jamaica. Practises such as face-to-face, one to one, and group counselling are common to the Jamaican scenario, in schools, churches, or elsewhere where career counselling takes place. These relationships based on trust are built between the counsellor and the client while the conditions and limitation of such relationships are expressed to the client. This approach essentially stemmed from Alfred Alder's theory of counselling and psychotherapy approach.

THE PROFESSIONAL ROLES AND RESPONSIBILITIES

It should be made particularly apparent that there is no separate distinction between the roles and responsibilities of a school counsellor. Seemingly, no understandable approach was identified to distinguish or separate what are roles, versus, what are responsibilities. What can be said however is that responsibilities are dependent on the type of role that a school counsellor has. The list of roles and responsibilities are in no way exhaustive. Therefore, we shall seek to identify and rationalise several key encompassing roles and responsibilities of school counsellors relating such specifically to the Jamaican school setting.

To accomplish our objective adequately and comprehensively, we first identify and define the key terms. The Compact Oxford English Dictionary (2006) defines rationalise as a justification for an action or attitude with logical reasoning. It further defines a role as a person's or thing's function in a particular situation. Responsibility is deemed as "a thing which one is required to do as part of a job, role, or legal obligation. [3]" School Counsellors are "professional members of an educational team who assists students in their personal, social and academic, and career development aspects of education through services such as individual counselling, small group counselling, and classroom teaching, and provide leadership in educational reform (advocacy)[4];"

---

3 http://www.askoxford.com/concise_oed/orexxsponsibility?view=uk

4 http://en.wiktionary.org/wiki/school_counselor

Roles of School Counsellor

The role of the School Guidance Counsellor is to act as an advocate for all students and to develop, co-ordinate and implement a school guidance program that assists all students (directly and indirectly) with personal and social growth, as well as educational and career development.[5] Another major role of the school counsellor would be to learn the counselling needs of students with disabilities and their parents (Hosie, 1982).

Although school counselling is a relatively new phenomenon to the Jamaican Landscape, we often do not understand or appreciate what duties school counsellors perform. The post of the School Counsellor was permanently established as part of the staffing structure of Secondary and High schools back in 1974. The

---

[5] http://chignecto-3.ednet.ns.ca/studentServicesManual/content/roles/content.asp?filename=guidanceCounsellor.htm

creation of the post arose out of the necessity to provide guidance to graduates of the newly created junior secondary schools. We cannot detail all the roles of school counsellors within this document; however, we will attempt to rationalize the school counsellor's roles.

Within our Jamaican schools, the school counsellor's primary role is to assist each child and his or her parents in mapping out the most appropriate educational program to ensure effective career plans and to facilitate life-long learning, good decision-making skills, and goal setting. Counsellors help select courses and programs that will best fit the student's abilities and interests and at the same time provide him or her with learning challenges. The school counsellors and other school personnel work collaboratively within the school environment in a positive way that helps students to succeed academically. School counsellors provide support for teachers by coordinating and implementing such activities.

The role of the school counsellor became necessary consequent to "the drug sub-culture, the perennial problem of teenage pregnancies, the need for career guidance and the absolute necessity for school welfare programmes" (Caenwood, 2000). Since then, the demands placed on Counsellors has doubled and has become more complex as the number of social problems in Jamaica has increased. Between 1974 and now, the Counsellor has assumed increasingly more responsibilities. Serving as a leader by sponsoring student activities, such as peer mediation, or school-wide initiatives, such as character education, school counsellors lessen the possibility of negative student behaviour which may lead to truancy, drug abuse, teenage pregnancy and or indiscipline. School counsellors are leaders in identifying and removing barriers to high academic achievement as they influence others to create a shared commitment to the common purpose of identifying oneself and accomplishing educational goals. The counsellor 's role is facilitative, non-judgemental, confidential, goal-oriented, and change-focused. He or she is "expected to function as a senior member of staff, answerable only to the senior administrators but more often directly to the Principal" (Caenwood, 2000).

One of the goals of a school counselling program is to enhance and promote student learning. Students who are experiencing such emotional traumas as relationship difficulties, personal and/or family crisis are not in the best mental state to engage in classroom learning. Often, classroom teachers do not have the skill or the time to help these students. Therefore, school counsellors help to enhance and promote student learning when students feel that their concerns are being listened to and understood, and when they receive help to overcome and move beyond such issues. Students feeling such support and help can cope with the learning demands of the classroom.

Credentials of the School Counsellor

Most professionals are guided by ethical standards for which their members may be held accountable and professional practice improved. Relatively young professions such as school counselling, develop these standards over time and they become systematized in codes. From these standards and guidelines, the responsibilities that govern school counsellors are derived. In Jamaican schools, counsellors are guided by the National Guidance Policy developed by the Ministry of Education and school programmes are designed based on the National Guidance Curriculum. Recent developments in the Jamaica Association of Guidance Counsellors in Education (JAGCE) suggest that in time the local profession will develop an internationally regarded code of ethics, which could become binding for all school counsellors.

The issue of Jamaican school counsellors being guided by the National Guidance Policy, which was developed by the Ministry of Education, is on the agenda of both the Ministry of Education and the Jamaica Association of Guidance Counsellors in Education (JAGCE). Ministry officials conduct periodic appraisals of counsellors employed in schools with a view of monitoring counsellor activity and performance in the field. The JAGCE has undertaken an initiative to partner with the US-based National Board for Certified Counsellors (NBCC) in developing and establishing a NBCC credential for Jamaica. When this agreement is complete the NBCC will provide certification for suitably qualified counsellors in Jamaica.

Responsibilities of a School Counsellor

Jamaican school counsellors have numerous responsibilities; several are identified below:

1. Co-ordinate all preventive and developmental programmes in the school (e.g., Career education, AIDS, and Drug prevention).
2. Organize and implement staff development training and identify suitable resource persons to implement this.
3. Assist/co-ordinate the school-feeding programme
4. Co-ordinate student welfare programme to include fund-raising activities.
5. Co-ordinate the prefect or student leadership activity within the school

6. Detect students with special needs and arranges for appropriate assistance
7. Liaise with referral agencies to address individual student's needs
8. Provide principal and staff with direction on student's social development and supply information for student recommendation and transcripts
9. Compile, organize and secure student confidential records
10. Establish and maintain the home-school link through planned home visits

Legal and Ethical Responsibilities

Presently school counsellors practicing in Jamaica, do so within the constraints of Jamaica law. The laws, which impinge directly upon a school counsellor's operation, are the

Education Act 1980 and its regulations and the Child Care and Protection Act 2004. The former governs the operations of schools in Jamaica. The latter reaffirms that children are the subjects of rights and that individuals and institutions in society are duty bound to ensure that these rights are promoted, protected, and upheld. Under this Act, it becomes mandatory for persons, namely school counsellors, with information of neglect or abuse of children to report such situations to relevant authorities (Caenwood, 2000).

Responsibilities to Students

The professional school counsellor has a primary obligation to the student, who is to be treated with respect as a unique individual[6]. This ensures and encourages the self-esteem and confidence of that student. In treating the individual with respect, the counsellor is

---

[6] http://www.schoolcounselor.org/content.asp?contentid=173

therefore enforcing and upholding the basic right and constitution of the individual. The counsellor is also concerned with the educational, academic, career, personal and social needs and encourages the maximum development of every student. It is the responsibility of the counsellor to act as facilitator/overseer, the one who ensures if no one else does, that the child is receiving education and that they grow as a complete and healthy human being. In addition, this allows the counsellor to identify the specific needs of this 'unique' child and in most cases train, coach, and teach them.

Another responsibility of the school counsellor is to respect the student's values and beliefs and do not impose their (the counsellor's) personal values. This is compulsory because every individual have a right and freedom to possess their own belief. They should be informed that they (the student) have a right to express their beliefs. The counsellor should advise the student that they too should respect other's differences and diverse nature. Knowledge of the laws, regulations and policies is compulsory as it relates to students, and counsellor must strive to protect and inform students regarding their rights. Without knowledge, we cannot function and perform our tasks. If the counsellor does not know what atrocities are being committed against a student, then he/she will not be able to protect them.

The school counsellor must inform students of the purposes, goals, techniques, and rules of procedure under which they may receive counselling at or before the time when the counselling relationship is entered. Disclosure notice includes the limits of confidentiality such as the possible necessity for consulting with other professionals, privileged communication, and legal or authoritative restraints. The meaning and limits of confidentiality are defined in developmentally appropriate terms to students. This is an integral function, because of the ethical and moral guidelines that govern the counsellor as he or she may be held liable for their actions if found in violation of any of the standards. Therefore, the child must be informed before the Counselling session begins, that the counsellor is obligated to disclose certain information if the actions of the student will bring harm to himself or to another. Also, if the child is being abused or threaten by anyone, this information must be shared with the relevant authorities.

Counselling Plans Responsibilities

The professional school counsellor provides students with a comprehensive school counselling program that includes a strong emphasis on working jointly with all students to develop academic and career goals. The counsellor also advocates for counselling plans supporting student's right to choose from the wide array of options when they leave secondary education. Such plans will be regularly reviewed to update students regarding critical information they need to make informed decisions. The counsellor does this to appropriately prepare the student for the working world and open their eyes to job possibilities. He/she must also ensure that they are informed about the jobs that suit their needs, interest, and skills.

Dual Relationships Responsibilities

Avoiding dual relationships that might impair his/her objectivity and increase the risk of harm to the student is a primary responsibility of the counsellor. If a dual relationship is unavoidable, the counsellor is responsible for taking action to eliminate or reduce the potential for harm. Such safeguards might include informed consent, consultation, supervision, and documentation. For a counsellor it is vital that dual relationships are reduced as much as possible, as the individual may be less likely to open up or disclose information that will allow them to be assisted. The avoidance of dual relationship will help the counsellor to eliminate preconceived notions of the individual, thereby, allowing fair treatment. The school counsellor must also avoid dual relationships with school personnel that might infringe on the integrity of the counsellor/student relationship. Persons should not view the counsellor in a manner which may detract from his function or credibility. There should be no issues that preoccupy their minds and cause them not to open up or feel safe with the counsellor.

Referral Responsibilities

Making referrals when necessary or appropriate to outside resources is another responsibility of the counsellor. Appropriate referrals may necessitate informing both parents/guardians and students of applicable resources and making proper plans for transitions with minimal interruption of services. Students retain the right to discontinue the counselling relationship at any time. The counsellor may not be able or is not equipped to deal with an issue. The counsellors aim and focus is always for the well-being of the student, therefore referral ensures that the student gets the best help possible. As the counselling relationship does not last forever, whenever further assistance is required, some support or resources should be identified to help the child.

Group Work Responsibilities

Counsellor's screen prospective group members and maintain an awareness of participants' needs and goals in relation to the goals of the group. The counsellor takes reasonable precautions to protect members from physical and psychological harm resulting from interaction within the group. Based on the ethical standards to uphold the main function of preventing harm to the child, the counsellor is responsible if they do not disclose to relevant authorities. Counsellors also notify parents/guardians and staff of group participation if the counsellor deems it appropriate and if consistent with school board policy or practice. This is done to make others, aware that the student is receiving help, let them know where the child is and gain permission from guardian.

Establishing clear expectations in the group setting and clearly stating that confidentiality in group counselling cannot be guaranteed is another task of the school counsellor. This is done to reiterate the need for privacy and to reassure others that nothing will be said. Given the developmental and chronological ages of minors in schools, the counsellor recognizes the tenuous nature of confidentiality for minors renders some topics inappropriate for group work in a school setting. The counsellor must follow up with group members and document proceedings as appropriate to ensure methods used were effective and the problem will not recur.

Summary

As stated, the roles and responsibilities of school counsellors cannot be adequately separated, as such they have been presented in such a manner as to allow the reader to draw his/her own conclusion. The role of the School Guidance Counsellor is to act as an advocate for all students while implementing a school guidance program that assists all students. As such there are numerous tasks and functions which they perform such as assist/co-ordinate the school-feeding programme, co-ordinate student welfare programmes to include fund-raising activities, co-ordinate the prefect or student leadership activity within the school, identify students with special needs and arrange appropriate assistance as well as liaise with referral agencies to address individual student's needs.

School counsellors practicing in Jamaica, do so within the constraints of Jamaica law which impinge directly upon a school counsellor's operation such as the Education Act 1980 and its regulations and the Child Care and Protection Act 2004. There is currently a partnership being created with the Ministry of Education and the Jamaica Association of Guidance Counsellors in Education (JAGCE) along with the US-based National Board for Certified Counsellors (NBCC) in developing and establishing a NBCC credential for Jamaica. These activities are geared to further formalise the roles and responsibilities of school counsellors operating within the Jamaican context.

PROFESSIONAL ORGANIZATIONS

Guidance counsellors were commonplace in American high schools, by the early 1950s and even emerged in some elementary school systems. Guidance counsellors were rife in colleges and universities. Guidance supervisors were being trained and had their own state organizations. In 1952, several state Guidance Supervisor and Guidance Trainers associations merged with the American College Personnel Association and the National Vocational Guidance Association to form the America Personnel and Guidance Association. That same year, the American School Counsellor Association (ASCA) became a founding division. APGA adopted ethical standards for its members in 1959. APGA changed its name to the American Association for Counselling and Development (AACD) in 1985 and to the American Counselling Association (ACA) in 1992. ACA reached membership more than 60,000 and as of 2003 had state branches in every state and many divisions representing specialties within the counselling profession[7].

On becoming a member of a professional organization, one may profit from social, economic, moral, personal, and intellectual benefits. Rogers's theory of self identifies two basic tenets, one of which refers to self-actualization. To be self-actualized as per Rogers's self-theory, a person may join a professional organization to have a sense of belonging - you no longer feel autonomous.

Members of professional organizations or associations influence the development of any profession by continuous efforts to improve specialized practices, services, and research. There is a professional association for almost any career field you can mention and joining

---

7 http://cmhs.utoledo.edu/mritchie/Courses/cmhs5010/unit02/history_of_school_counseling.htm

them will ensure that one can partake of the benefits. If you want to do something great for your future job hunt and your career, become a member of a Professional Association.

Professional associations publish journals and/or newsletters (which often are a benefit of membership). These are helpful to keep you up to date on issues and developments in your field. If you are interviewing, this can be invaluable information. Secondly, you will identify the "movers and shakers" in your field. Also, you will learn about the companies or individuals with whom you would like to work. Information about upcoming conferences and professional development opportunities will be more accessible (Kearsley, 2004).

With your membership, you will often have access to member information (*ACPI, 2004)*). Contacting someone in your field about possible employment as a fellow member of the association may open a door. Professional associations often have some mechanism for sharing job listings. This could be a "classified" section in the journal or newsletter, a section on a web site, or a separate publication available to members only. As a member, you will be eligible to attend the group's conferences. These conferences offer excellent opportunities to build your network of professionals in the field, learn the latest developments in your field, and take professional courses and seminars (ACSCI, 2004).

Professional membership is also an excellent addition to your resume. There are few better ways to show your serious commitment to the field. Local chapters of associations often sponsor programs, maintain alumni networks, and provide other valuable advantages. Many professional associations have substantially reduced membership fees for students who are still in college. Fees can get a little pricey if one waits until after you graduate. If an individual wants to do their future a favour, they should seek out and join the professional association in their area of career interest.

It is important to join a Professional Association. Its value will unfold and may affect your career and of course it will probably be the best decision one can make for your future. The benefits will include being able to have a voice in decisions that affect your practice. Also, you will be able to meet your needs for life-long learning. Information regarding your profession will be more accessible. However, most importantly, you will be able to distinguish yourself as a professional.

After joining and following a professional body, one may have advantages in the social, economic, personal, and other realms of your life. These may present themselves in different ways, whether your discipline would be increased, or your morals and intellectual values would have benefited positively from the organization's principles. As cited from A Longo, "Never doubt that a small group of thoughtful, committed people can change the world. Indeed, it is the only thing that ever has."

The NCDA ethical standards

To examine ethical standards of the National Career Development Association (NCDA) we must first understand what ethics is, then one will be able to apply the knowledge of it to better scrutinize the given topic.

According to Dorothy C. Wertz, Ethics is a field of human inquiry ("science" according to some definitions) that examines the bases of human goals and the foundations of "right" and "wrong" human actions that further or hinder these goals.

We may not think about it every day, but we all depend on the ethical behaviour of our co-workers, our immediate supervisors, and higher levels of management. The daily decisions we all make affect our future and the future of others. We are all parts of a system in which each part has the potential to affect all other parts either positively or negatively.

A society without ethics is a society doomed to extinction. Basic concepts and theories of ethics provide the framework necessary for working out one's own moral or ethical code. In our field "if you lose your reputation of being an honest person, you have lost your reputation of being a good accountant." (Dr. Leon Woodfield). Our response to ethical situations moulds and shapes our character and determines the type of person we will be in the future.

On a personal level most, people feel better working for an ethical organization. If the organization truly values fairness, honesty, and integrity, employees are more likely to enjoy their work and take pride in the organization. At the professional level ethically oriented codes of conduct are common. Professions recognize that their credibility rests not only on technical competence, but also on public trust. At the organizational level, ethics is good business. As cited by Sally Kearsley, several studies have shown that over the long run ethical businesses do better than unethical businesses.

Ethics enables people to think for themselves, and to consider interests of all parties concerned. It is also important because private decisions may lead to cultural transformations. Ethics helps us to look beyond the details of the immediate situation. Now that we understand the definition of ethics and its objectives, we will now examine the first five guidelines under section B: Counselling Relationship and discuss their importance as it pertains to the effectiveness of career counselling.

Section B: Counselling Relationship

The primary obligation of the Career counsellor is to respect the integrity and promote the welfare of the client. This means that whatever physical or psychological trauma a client is going through it is the Career Counsellor's responsibility to protect his/her client. For example, in a school setting where a student is having sexual relations with her father and the school counsellor is aware of the problem and is working with the student. The counsellor has the right to report the issue to the proper authorities. However, the responsibility encompasses that of not making the situation worse, whether by causing the child's school experience or other social environment to become overwhelming and initially harmful to her physically, emotionally, or socially.

It is further stated in Section B. No. 2 guideline that the counsellor relationship and information must remain confidential. This is very important base on the legal and ethical aspect of the counsellor and client relationship in whatever setting the counselling may take. In other words, a counsellor cannot go and publish or broadcast his client's situation all over town. This would not only be unethical but also unprofessional.

No. 3 guideline states that counsellors consider the traditions and practices of the other professional groups. This statement indicates that in the case where a client is receiving counselling another counsellor should not take on this individual until it is communicated among them, or the client is referred to another counsellor. This reduces the risk of confusion and conflict and promotes the 1st guideline.

The fourth guideline refers to a condition that indicates the presence of a clear and imminent danger to the client or other. The counsellor must take reasonable action or inform responsible person(s) or government bodies. If it is an instance where another counsellor is better able to assist it should then be referred to that professional. However, in acting on the problem the counsellor must be careful of how this may affect the client's behaviour. In a situation where there is reason to think that the client is violent, or that is he or she is a threat to society, or even to the counsellor; it is the counsellor's responsibility to find techniques and method to counteract that behaviour. This may be done by consulting with another professional as well as observing caution before taking matters in his or her hands. To carry out these measures, client participation is always required.

The last guideline addresses the matter of records as it relates to personal information for clients. If record keeping takes the form of interview notes, test data, correspondence, audio, or visual tape recordings, and other documents; these are to be considered professional information. It is so important that records be kept confidential to protect the client interest. Even in the case where a counsellor needs information on a particular client, he/she must get consent from that individual. Many counsellors perform public speech to peers or supervisors and often refer to their cases as examples. It is the responsibility of that counsellor to keep his/her information in general so as not to disclose any specific information about his/her clients. Even though the information is general in these settings it should be accurate and unbiased.

There is a popular Christian joke of a priest and a politician. The politician was late for the meeting, and the catholic priest went up trying to buy some time. The spoke of his first confessional and gave details of how this gentleman had robbed a bank, killed someone, and cheated on his wife. When the politician finally arrived, he started to tell the gathering that he was the first person this priest had in confession. This is just an example of how detrimental it is to share specific information. This should be kept confidential between a counsellor and a client.

Summary

Each guideline is imperative to the effective performance of a career counsellor. Initially we had defined and discussed what ethics was and based on the information presented, we understood that ethical guidelines assist us in maintaining what is right. It sets a common code by which all individuals are judged and deemed credible. Ethical standards also promote the growth of companies, groups, or associations. We each live by a biblical guideline 'Treat others as you would have them treat you.' Ethical standards are the foundation that trust is built on between a counsellor and a client.

Do the ethical codes laid down by the NCDA in section B: Counselling Relationship mirrors the objective of what an ethical guide should be? Yes. Do the standards present a 'bar' by which one can be deemed credible and penalised if found to be breaking these rules? Yes. Do they have the client's interest and well being at heart? Yes. Do they aim to protect and prevent any arm that may affect the counselling relationship? Yes. Lastly, and most importantly, do these guidelines promote trust? Yes.

It is our belief that the first five guidelines of section B: Counselling Relationship, of the NCDA standards, fulfils the requirement of a true and upholding standard. They meet the objectives laid down at the definition and promote what ethics is all about. It is also our belief that without these codes, there would be serious repercussions throughout the counselling arena. Without ethical guideline, the world of counselling would be doomed.

RESOURCES

The Guidance and Counselling Unit

The Guidance and Counselling Unit ensures that the school facilities which are in place are effectively utilised for the total development of the individual student, to enable him or her to lead a more fulfilling life. The unit develops services and programmes for the personal/social, educational, and career development of all students. In addition, the unit coordinates the training and development of counsellors in schools and is responsible for several programmes including the HIV/AIDS Programme in Schools, the Programme for Alternative Student Support, the Safe Schools Programme and the Health and Family Life Education in Schools.

For further information please contact the:
Ministry of Education
Guidance and Counselling Unit
Caenwood Centre
37 Arnold Road
Kingston 5
Telephone: (876) 967-0146

Women's Centre of Jamaica Foundation

The Women's Centre of Jamaica Foundation (WCJF) is a limited liability company under the auspices of the Office of the Prime Minister. One of its priorities, the programme for Adolescent Mothers, is aimed at assisting pregnant girls, 17 and under to continue their secondary education. Under the programme, girls who have dropped out of school due to pregnancy can continue their education at the Women's Centres nearest to them for at least one term and are subsequently returned to the formal school system after the birth of their babies.

For further information please contact them at:
Telephone: (876) 929-7608, 929-0977
Email: womenscentre@cwjamaica.com
Website: http://www.jamaica-kidz.com/womenscentre/

Family Life Ministries Jamaica

Family Life Ministries is a non-denominational, Bible-based organization with the purpose of developing and providing a range of ministries related to all aspects of family life. They are a non-profit, non-shareholding organization which was established in 1982 out of the recognition that the deterioration of family life was an area in urgent need of redress. Their goal is, therefore, the improvement and development of family life and interpersonal relationships.

They offer:

1. Individual Counselling
2. Marital Counselling
3. Family Counselling
4. General Counselling

For further information please contact them at:
Address: 1 Cecelio Avenue, Kingston 10 Jamaica
Phone: (876) 926-8101; 929-4360
Email: fam.life@cwjamaica.com
Web: www.familylifeministriesjamaica.com

Peer Counselling Association of Jamaica (PCAJ)

The Peer Counselling Association of Jamaica (PCAJ) was established in 1990, under the umbrella of the Kingston and St. Andrew Family Life Planning Project, funded by the United Nations Population Fund (UNFPA). The Peer Counselling Association of Jamaica (PCAJ) is a voluntary grassroots organization which provides Life skills Training, Parenting Education and Peer Counselling Programmes in various schools and communities across Jamaica. The organisation is organized exclusively to promote and advance the dissemination of Sexual and Reproductive Health information with respect to the training of persons (regardless of sex, age, or class) in life coping skills with special emphasis on and to provide educational and support counselling in sexual reproductive health.

Address: 2c Halsey Avenue, Kingston 3
Phone: (876) 928-9111; 841-4426
Fax: (876) 622-7212
Email: pcajam@netscape.net
Web Site: http://orgs.takingitglobal.org/2176

Ministry of Justice Victim Support Unit

The VSU seeks to provide opportunity for healing and therapeutic intervention to assist the Ministry to balance justice for all victims of crime. This mandate is carried out through our fourteen (14) parish offices island wide. The Victim Support Programme (VSP) was established to address the numerous needs of victims of crime. It was also intended that the programme of support for victims in Jamaica, be developed as a partnership between the government and the community.

For further information please contact them at:
Address: 47E Old Hope Road, Kingston 5
Telephone: (876) 946 – 0663; 946 – 9287; 927 - 8416

National Council on Drug Abuse

The National Council on Drug abuse was established in October 1983. When the NCDA was established, it was charged with the responsibility of educating the public about the dangers of drug use, and of preventing the indiscriminate use of drugs. Since then, however, the Council has had to review its role, and this has led to an expansion of its terms of reference to include an examination of the legal, medical and security issues surrounding drug abuse, as well as research.

The NCDA has formulated projects to address all the various key elements and established a comprehensive national policy on drug abuse prevention policy for demand and supply reduction.

For further information please contact them at:
National Council on Drug Abuse
2-6 Melmac Avenue
Kingston 5, Jamaica
Telephone: 1-888-991-4244

National Family Planning Board (NFPB)

The National Family Planning Board is a statutory agency of the Ministry of Health, Jamaica. The organization is empowered to prepare, carry out and promote the carrying out of family and family life education programmes in Jamaica. The mission of the National Family Planning Board is, to play a leading role in identifying, developing, promoting and co-ordinating national policies and programmes that recognize the rights of the individual to high quality family planning services appropriate to their reproductive health needs and status, in keeping with Government objectives and the international environment.

For further information please contact them at:
Address: P.O. Box 287 5 Sylvan Avenue, Kingston 5
Phone Number: 968-1627, 968- 1629, 968 - 1631, 968 - 1633, 968 - 1636
Email: jnfpb@jnfpb.org
Website: http://www.jnfpb.org/

Women's Resource and Outreach Centre (WROC)

WROC aims to provide holistic services and programmes that promote gender equality and the empowerment of women and youth. These services and programmes are rooted in the attainment of women's rights as described in the Convention on the Elimination of All Forms of Discrimination Against Women (CEDAW) as well as the achievement of the Millennium Development Goals (MDGs), to which Jamaica is a signatory. This is accomplished through the work of four focus areas or clusters: Health and Wellness, Sustainable Livelihoods, Advocacy, Research and Communications, Community Capacity-Building. Additionally, WROC engages in several collaborations with international and local donors as well as civil society organisations to accomplish its goals.

For further information please contact them at:
Address: 47 Beechwood Avenue, Kingston 5, Jamaica, W.I.

Telephone: (876) 929-8873 or (876) 960-9067
Fax: (876) 968-9260

REFERENCE

1. Oxford, (2006). Rationalise. Compact Oxford English Dictionary. http://www.askoxford.com/results/?view=dict&freesearch=Rationalise%20&branch=13842570&textsearchtype=exact

2. Oxford, (2006). Responsibility. Compact Oxford English Dictionary of Current English. http://www.askoxford.com/concise_oed/orexxsponsibility?view=uk

3. University of Toledo, (2006). A Brief History of School Counselling; http://cmhs.utoledo.edu/mritchie/Courses/cmhs5010/unit02/history_of_school_counseling.htm

4. (2006). America's Career Resource Network Association. http://www.acrna.net/index.htm

5. (2006). Association for Career and Technical Education. Retrieved from http://www.acteonline.org/join/index.cfm

6. (2006). Association of Career Professionals International. Retrieved from http://www.acpinternational.org/about/benefits.html

7. (2006). Association of Computer-based Systems for Career Information. http://www.acsci.org/acsci_join1.htm

8. Baker, S.B. (1992). School counselling for the twenty-first century. Upper Saddle River, NJ: Prentice-Hall.

9. Cunningham, T., Rowland K., (2006). Counselling in the School. http://www.valdosta.edu/schc/counseling%20in%20the%20school.pdf

10. Ethical Standards for School Counsellors, (2004). ASCA's Ethical Standards for School Counsellors. http://www.schoolcounselor.org/content.asp?contentid=173

11. Gordon- Rowe. N., (1997). Adolescence: Lecture Notes. G-Rowe Publications Ja.

12. Himel, M., (1999). A Student's Guide to Careers in the Helping Professions.

13. http://chignecto3.ednet.ns.ca/studentServicesManual/content/roles/content.asp?filename=guidanceCounsellor.htm

14. Wikipedia, (2006). School Counsellor. https://en.wikipedia.org/wiki/School_counselor

15. http://www.gnb.ca/0000/publications/ss/NBSchoolCounsellingREV.pdf

16. Kearsley, S., (2006). It Pays to Join a Professional Association. http://www.jobweb.com/Resources/Library/Career_Pursuit/It_Pays_to_Join_a_132_01.htm

17. NCDA, (2003). National Career Development Association Ethical Standards. www.ncda.org

18. Schmidt, J.J. (2003). Counselling in schools: Essential services and comprehensive programs. 4th ed. Boston: Allyn & Bacon

19. Wertz, D., (2004). Ethics: What is It and Why is It Important? A Primer for Non-Ethicists. http://www.umassmed.edu/shriver/research/socialscience/staff/wertz/ethics.cfm

20. Jamaica Educational System Overview. (2014). http://education.stateuniversity.com/pages/727/Jamaica-EDUCATIONAL-SYSTEM-OVERVIEW.html

21. MOE, (2014). Vision 2030 Jamaica National Development Plan, Education Draft Sector Plan. http://www.moe.gov.jm/node/16

22. (2015). A Personal view of counselling: http://pblib.utpb.edu/MARION/ABV-3976

23. (2015). Counselling. http://pblib.utpb.edu/MARION?S=COUNSELING

24. George, R., Cristiani, T., (1995). Counselling: Theory and Practice, 4th Ed. Allyn & Bacon, 1995.

25. Gladding, S., (1996). Counselling: A Comprehensive Profession. 5th Ed. New Jersey: Merrill Prentice Hall, 1996.

26. Hackney, H., Cormier, L., (1996). The Professional Counsellor: A Process to Helping, 3rd Ed. Allyn & Bacon, 1996.

27. The Counsellor and Counselling Process. http://www.wctc.edu/busocc/treatmentissues/08 Black/tsld055.htm

28. Chapman, A., (2005). Eric Berne's Transactional Analysis - early TA history and theory. http://www.businessballs.com/transact.htm

29. Davidson, C., Mountain, A., Chapman, A., (2005). Eric Berne's Transactional Analysis - TA theory development and explanation. http://www.businessballs.com/transactionalanalysis.htm

30. George, R., Cristiani, T., (1995). Counselling: Theory and Practice, (4th Ed). Allyn and Bacon.

31. Gibson, R., Mitchell, M., (1999). Introduction to Counselling and Guidance (5th Ed). Merrill Prentice Hall.

32. Gladding, S., (1996). Counselling: A Comprehensive Profession. (5th Ed). New Jersey: Merrill Prentice Hall, 2004.

33. Gladding, S., (2004). Counselling: A Comprehensive Approach. (5th Ed). New Jersey: Merrill Prentice Hall.

34. Hackney, H., Cormier, L., (1996). The Professional Counsellor: A Process to Helping, (3rd Ed). Allyn and Bacon.

35. Parsons, Richard D. (1994). Counselling Strategies and Intervention Techniques for the Human Services 4th ed.: Allyn and Bacon.

Remember, "the heights by great men reached and kept were not attained by sudden flight, but they, while their companions slept, were toiling upward in the night." – Henry Wadsworth Longfellow.

ABOUT THE AUTHOR

Denise N. Fyffe

… is an author, educator, and Christian minister whose understanding of workplace culture was shaped not in theory, but through years of lived experience inside Jamaican institutions, tertiary environments, and corporate learning spaces. Her professional journey has taken her through organizations with strong systems and those with fragile ones, giving her a front-row seat to the realities of workplace theft, leadership gaps, human behaviour, and the quiet emotional toll these issues leave behind.

Born and raised in Kingston, Jamaica, Denise carries the resilience, cultural insight, and grounded wisdom of the communities that shaped her—Harbour View, Windward Road, Rockfort, and Seaview Gardens. These early experiences taught her how people navigate pressure, how trust is built and broken, and how integrity becomes a daily practice rather than an abstract ideal.

With more than two decades of experience across education, training, publishing, and ministry, Denise has worked in environments where systems were strong and transparent, and in others where vulnerabilities created opportunities for misconduct. These contrasting realities deepened her understanding of organizational behaviour and inspired her commitment to helping institutions build cultures of trust, accountability, and protection.

She is the founder of RTCLM Ministry, RTCLM Academy and Foundation as well as Jamaica Pen Publishers; where she mentors writers, develops leaders, and creates resources that strengthen both individuals and organizations. Her work blends cultural awareness, spiritual grounding, and practical guidance, offering readers clarity in environments that often feel overwhelming or uncertain.

Across more than 90 published books, Denise has explored themes of emotional wellness, spiritual growth, family life, and personal resilience. In this book, she brings together her professional experience, her ministry perspective, and her lived encounters with workplace systems to offer a rare, honest, and deeply human look at integrity in the modern workplace.

Denise continues to write, teach, and minister with a heart for service and a commitment to helping people and organizations thrive with dignity, wisdom, and purpose.

RECOMMENDED BOOKS

THE
GLOBAL
FAMILY

THE
FAMILY

MODERN
FAMILY

THE
AMERICAN
FAMILY

THE
BLENDED
FAMILY

THE
PSYCHOLOGY
of
WORKPLACE
THEFT
DENISE N. FYFFE

DEVELOPING
PEOPLE
LEARNING
DENISE H. FYFFE

EMPOWERING
WORKER
DENISE H. FYFFE

THIEVES
WORKPLACE
DENISE H. FYFFE

THE IMPACT
LEARNING
MANAGEMENT
DENISE N. FYFFE

THE IMPACT
TRADE
UNIONS
Jamaica
DENISE N. FYFFE

UNDERSTANDING
the
ELEMENT
DENISE N. FYFFE

SOPHIE'S PLACE
DISABLED

THE
PHILOSOPHY
EDUCATION AND
WORK

THE GUIDANCE
COUNSELOR'S

All books are available at online book retailers.

Dear Reader

Thank you for reading this book.

It means so much that you have taken the time out of your busy schedule. Nothing makes us happier than knowing that someone is reading, and hopefully enjoying, what took us many months, even years, to create.

Please stay with us on this journey. We welcome your feedback, opinions, and suggestions about the book. We would appreciate a few lines of review on the website where you purchased this book.

You can also write us a note at Jamaica Pen Publishing on Facebook, or Twitter or contact us via our website.

www.ingramcontent.com/pod-product-compliance
Lightning Source LLC
La Vergne TN
LVHW022102200926
848481LV00003B/1047
9798232077976